D0904740

The Exemplary Husband

A Biblical Perspective

Revised Edition

By Stuart Scott

Study Guide

Study Guide
for
The Exemplary Husband
A Biblical Perspective
Revised Edition
by Dr. Stuart Scott

Copyright 2002 FOCUS PUBLISHING, INC.
All rights reserved

No part of this book may be reproduced by any means
without written consent of the publisher
except for brief quotes used in reviews written specifically
for use in a magazine or newspaper.

Unless otherwise noted, all Scripture is taken from
©   The New American Standard Bible
1960, 1962, 1963, 1971, 1973, 1977, 1995
by the Lockman Foundation
Used by permission

Cover design by Richard Schaefer

ISBN 1-885904-22-3

THE EXEMPLARY HUSBAND

Student Guide

Part One-A Husband's Recognitions
Foundational Truths for the Exemplary Husband

Part Two-A Husband's Responsibilities
Faithful Commitments of the Exemplary Husband

Part Three-A Husband's Resolves
Fundamental Commitments of the Exemplary Husband

Part Four-A Husband's Regrets
Fatal Sins to the Exemplary Husband

Chapter One

A Husband's Understanding of His Present Condition

The Exemplary Husband and this study guide focus on your walk with God and your character by examining what God's Word has to say to husbands. You as a husband must lead the way in seeking to build God's kind of marriage. You must be honest in looking at your heart in light of God's perfect standard. Self-examination and change can be a painful process as we see where we fall short of that standard. But when we make the effort needed, humbly submitting to His will, repenting of sin, and committing ourselves to live biblical lives, God will bless us and change us to be more like Christ. Be diligent, thoughtful, and prayerful as you answer these questions and meditate upon God's Word.

1. Have you ever been approached by your wife about an area of your life that does not measure up to God's standards? What was the issue and what was the outcome of your conversation?

    Stay up too late −.
    Change for a time, then revert back.

2. If you have never had this happen, ask your wife if she is aware of any areas of your marriage in which you do not measure up to God's standards (There is surely at least one!). Remember to be humble and honest at her response, even if she is less than compassionate in her remarks. Then describe the way in which you do not meet God's standards.

Recognizing her efforts/work enough.

3. Now read Psalm 51 and 2 Corinthians 7:9-11 and describe in your own words what kind of sorrow you should have and what you should think about those areas of your marriage that fall short of God's standards.

Sincere sorrow based on living outside God's word, but know that "Godly sorrow" can lead to legitimate change/good things.

4. Read 1 Corinthians 11:1; 1 John 2:3-6, and 2 Corinthians 3:18. According to these verses, what is the standard for your behavior? What is the word in Chapter One that summarizes this standard (other than "exemplary")?

    Christ - like

5. In what specific ways can you see yourself not walking "in the same manner as He walked" (1 John 2:6)? What changes do you need to make to fix these problems?

    • Greater involvement w/ those close to me
    • Better example/witness
    • More support for my wife

6. Write out your own definition of an exemplary husband using as much Scripture as possible to support your definition.

    To love, support + lead in all circumstances.

7. Chapter One states that any man can be an exemplary husband if four things are true of him. What are those four things?

    • Right relationship w/ God
    • Recognize that growth is needed
    • Follow the perfect example
    • Realize that sin is the only thing that can stand in your way.

8. Describe specifically ways in which you currently measure up to those four things or ways in which you don't measure up to them.

① Need long history of consistent quiet time
② I do recognize need for growth, that I have a long way to go.
③ Need to remember WWJD throughout day.
④ Need to remember that this is a battle I can only lose through sin.

9. Look at the chart on page six, and write out one sentence describing how you personally need to change to be like Christ in each of the six characteristics listed there.

I need to continue to be influenced more by Him + less by the world, but 'stay in the world' + learn to have a positive influence for Him.

10. Only sin stands in the way of your success in being an exemplary husband. What commitment are you willing to make before God that you will pursue holiness and godliness as a husband as you continue throughout the rest of this study and the rest of your life (1Timothy 4:7-9)?

I commit to win the battle!

Chapter Two

A Husband's Understanding of God

Understanding God is fundamental to becoming an exemplary husband. Men cannot lead their wives and families to know our great God without knowing Him themselves. A husband must first be in a right relationship with God before he can love his wife as he should. Holding to a faulty view of God will make it impossible to know Christ and build a life that resembles His. The questions below will help you examine what the Scriptures say about God and grow in your relationship with Him.

1. Read 2 Timothy 3:16-17. In your own words, describe why this passage is foundational to our study on how to be the exemplary husband.

   We should read His word that is God-breathed to learn how to get closer to God, continually improve our ability to know w/ confidence What Jesus would do.

2. Read John 1:1-3 and Colossians 1:15-18. What do these two passages teach us about Jesus Christ?

   Jesus has been w/ the Father from the beginning. Thate He made all things + is in all things.

3. Foundational to being the exemplary husband is having a solid foundation in your relationship to God. Describe in your own words at least two of the popular views of God described in this chapter. Focus on those which you may have had in the past or still have to some extent.

① Domesticated genie ~ If you are good, you will be rewarded, completely based on your own works

② Ogre ~ God punishes based on your bad deeds or wrong things said.

Both to some extent ~ In the past I thought I could do it all w/out Jesus, based on my own abilities.

4. Read each of the following passages and describe in your own words what it says God is like and what our relationship with God is to be like.

a) Romans 11:35-36
He can't repay, he has no debt to anyone. To Him belong all things

b) Matthew 7:9-11
Ask & you will receive (Father→Son)

c) Romans 8:32
God gave up his Son, what could he possibly be NOT willing to give.

d) Isaiah 46:9-10
The Only God. All powerful.

e) Lamentations 3:31-33

He may discipline, but shows compassion/love always.

f) Psalm 145:8-9

God loves first, is slow to anger.

g) Psalm 100:2-3

Know God made us, that we belong to him.

h) Revelation 4:11

God is worthy of our praise, He created all things.

i) Isaiah 46:11

j) Psalm 33:13-15

k) Deuteronomy 6:4-5; 2 Samuel 7:22; John 17:3

l) Psalm 50:21

m) Exodus 15:11

n) Psalm 7:11

o) Psalm 103:9-11

p) Psalm 10:15

q) Hebrews 4:14-16

r) Psalm 23:1; John 10:14-15

s) 1 John 3:1-3; Romans 8:1-4; Ephesians 1:5-6

t) Hebrews 12:6

u) Romans 8:38-39; Deuteronomy 7:9

v) Ecclesiastes 12:13-14

w) Matthew 16:24

x) Luke 6:46

y) Jeremiah 9:23-24

5. Now write out in your own words what God is like based upon the verses you just wrote about in the previous questions.

6. Finally, write out a definition of what your relationship with God should be based upon and what it should be like.

Chapter Three

A Husband's Understanding of Man and Sin

There is no end to opinions about what we are, what our purpose in life is, and what we need to be happy. But the source of truth about man is not sociology, psychology, or secular anthropology, and certainly not a magazine article or the host of some television show! Only God's perfect and Holy Word can guide us into this truth. We need to closely examine what the Bible says about mankind, what our needs truly are, and the provisions God has made to meet those needs.

1. Read Romans 12:3. Specifically apply this verse to yourself.

   Be honest in measuring yourself. -Measure by how much faith God has given you

2. In this chapter, several false views of man were discussed. Briefly describe each false view and use Scripture to demonstrate the error of each view. (See also Study Guide Appendix 2.)

   a) Man is basically good at heart.

   Our nature is sinful. The more we know God's word/law, the more we know that we aren't obeying it

   Romans 3:9-20

b) Man is evolving or getting better and better as time goes by.

As we move further away from God, we become MORE sinful.

c) Man can be good enough to please God.

His standard is perfection, we cannot get there.

d) Man is just a victim of his circumstances. *Job! Paul!*

We will be held accountable regardless of circumstances.

If you truly know God, you can lead the life God wants you to lead despite the circumstances.

3. What are the four wrong ideas associated with the word "victim" (see also Study Guide Appendix 2)?

① Complete innocence implied, which often isn't the case.

② Implies that a senseless event happened — it never should have happened. This ignores God's sovereign plan.

③ Often gives a person a hopeless outlook.

④ Usually allows a person to ignore personal responsibility.

4. Does a "victim mentality" manifest itself in any areas of your life? If so, write down which wrong ideas are producing that kind of thinking, and which truths from God's Word should replace them (see also Study Guide Appendix 2).

• Work, I sometimes give up too easily.

5. The key to understanding who we really are is to understand ourselves in relationship to God our Creator. Use at least two passages from the Bible to demonstrate that man has been created by God and is therefore both totally dependent upon Him and necessarily subordinate to Him.

Gen 1:27, Psalm 24:1   Ps 113:4-6

We didn't make the world! We are made in his image, but are NOT like him.

6. Name at least three reasons Scripture gives us for God's creation of man. How do each of these apply to our standing before God and how we should live?

· Created for God by God.

· To worship him, to be His people, to Glorify Him
    (To put his character on display)

7. Explain why the Bible states that man is now by nature an enemy of God. Use at least two passages from the Bible to prove this point.

· Sin   · Isaiah 59:2 - Sin separates us from God
             · Romans 1:18-25 Creating NEW ways to sin.

8. Today it is very popular to focus on our "needs," but the Bible has a very different idea of what our real needs are. Give at least two real needs of man according to the Scriptures expounded in this chapter. Then, list any errant "needs" views you may have had before reading this chapter and explain why they are not biblical.

· Walk w/ God in His truth   · Needs God to Act

9. Write out, in a couple of sentences each, at least three provisions that God has made to satisfy our true needs.

- Salvation: God paid for OUR sins through Jesus on the Cross.

- Sanctification: We are not immediately all that we should be once saved. We are given resources (Bible, Holy Spirit, Church) to continue to grow.

- Glorification: We will see Jesus in Heaven! We must strive to always walk w/ Him, because our actions come from our motives/beliefs/thoughts.

10. Write out a definition from the chapter explaining the biblical process of change. (See also Appendix 2 in *The Exemplary Husband*.)

Striving to become more Christlike everyday by reading the Bible, fellowship @ church and listening to the Holy Spirit.

11. Apply this definition to at least one area of your life. Be specific with both the "put off" and the "put on" and exert maximum effort in your life and marriage to be more like Christ in this area. (Use the "Put Off-Put On" chart in Study Guide Appendix 3 to do this.)

Chapter Four

A Husband's Understanding of Relationships

Both society and the Church suffer from a lack of understanding about relationships. But God is concerned about relationships and has given us much instruction about how to fulfill His will in relating to Him and others. Relationships are not static things; they are either getting worse or getting better. They take work! As you answer the questions below, consider whether you are putting forth the effort necessary to make sure all the relationships in your life are growing, especially the two most important ones, with God and with your wife.

1. Write out a biblical definition of what a relationship is.

2. In what way have we been created dependent and interdependent? Why is it false to think of ourselves as being independent?

3. How is God Himself the blueprint for what a relationship is to be like? Be specific and demonstrate this using several Scriptures.

4. In what way can we never model ourselves after God in terms of relationship? Why can't we ever attain that? Use Scripture to prove this point.

5. What is the difference between a mutual relationship and a non-mutual relationship? What is your responsibility in a non-mutual relationship?

6. Write out a couple of sentences defining the five stated major pitfalls in relationships as listed in the chapter. Then, take time to evaluate your self against each one, particularly in regards to your relationship with your Creator and then your wife. Describe in detail ways that you have stumbled into these particular pitfalls.

7. Now write out a plan for biblical change with any areas uncovered in the previous question.

Notes

Chapter Five
A Husband's Understanding of Marriage

If you took a survey and asked people to give one word that sums up marriage for them, you'd probably hear words like "conflict," "boring," and "unfulfilling." But none of these answers describes what God created marriage to be. The Bible has a lot to say about God's intentions for marriage. What you think about marriage will affect your perspective of your role, your wife's role, and the marriage itself. Commit yourself to be instructed by God's Word on this important topic.

1. As stated in the chapter, God created marriage for the purpose of companionship. List in the Study Guide ways that you as a husband can treat your wife more as a companion than you have in the past. Be specific.

2. God created the wife to be a helper to her husband. List in the Study Guide ways that your wife already works as a helper to you. Be specific and observant.

3. What is a key pitfall to guard against in your understanding of your wife as a helper?

4. In what sense has God created marriage for procreation?

5. Describe in detail the biblical commandment of Genesis 2:24 as it relates to marriage in general, and then as it relates to your marriage. Are there any ways in which you need to change in your personal relationships to more faithfully obey God's commandment of Genesis 2:24?

6. In what sense has God created marriage as an illustration? What role are you as the husband to play in this illustration? Specifically, how are you to fulfill this role to your own wife?

7. What does Matthew 19:6 teach about the marriage relationship?

8. Write out at least three ways in which marriage is to be a sanctifying or perfecting relationship. Include at least three Scripture passages to demonstrate this.

Notes

Chapter Six

A Husband's Understanding of His Role

There are many views today about the nature of man and woman, from the extremes of the male chauvinist to the militant feminist. With all the confusion regarding the differences between men and women, we need to look at what God says about the matter. He has clearly described in His Word what He designed men and women to be, particularly in their roles as husbands and wives.

1. In what way are husband and wife equal? Write a couple of sentences explaining each way.

2. In what way are husband and wife unequal? Write a couple of sentences to clearly explain the answer.

3. What are the four key features of Christlike leadership listed in the chapter?

4. Think of several areas in which you are not leading your wife properly. What do you need to do to change these areas?

5. Read each of the following verses and briefly explain what each one says about how you should love your wife.

    a) Ephesians 5:25

    b) Ephesians 5:28-29

    c) Colossians 3:19

6. As the chapter says, you must love your wife sacrificially, actively, and according to knowledge. What are some ways in which you are not living up to this standard in your marriage? What do you need to do to change?

Chapter Seven

A Husband's Responsibility
Worshiping Christ Only

Perhaps when you think of idolatry you only think of graven images or the gods of false religion. In Ezekiel 14:1-11, God pointedly addresses another kind of idol—an idol of the heart. Ezekiel speaks about some of the elders of Israel who had "set up idols in their heart" (v. 3). In fact, it mentions the possibility of a "multitude" of idols in one heart (v. 4). From this we learn that we can be engaged in idolatry, even though we are not physically bowing down to someone or something. In his commentary on 1 Corinthians, John MacArthur writes:

> Idolatry includes much more than bowing down or burning incense to a physical image. Idolatry is having any false god—any object, idea, philosophy, habit, occupation, sport, or whatever that has one's primary concern and loyalty to the Lord. (The MacArthur New Testament Commentary, 1 Corinthians, Chicago: Moody Press, 1984, pp. 232-233)

1. Read Deuteronomy 10:12-14, 20-21. What does God say are the characteristics of a worshiping heart?

2. The chapter says that the heart is almost the same as the mind. Read Proverbs 23:7; Matthew 13:15, and Mark 2:6. Write out the phrase in each of these verses that proves this to be true.

3. List five attitudes or activities (given in the chapter) that characterize true worship of God. Of those five, which ones characterize your heart the least? What do you need to do to sharpen the focus of your heart in these areas?

4. According to the chapter, what are the three ways you make something an idol in your heart?

5. Look at your life in light of the answer to #4. Describe at least one idol that you currently have in your life.

6. What are the four ways in which God reveals our idolatrous lusts to us and convicts us of idolatry?

7. A refuge is something we turn to other than God when our hearts have stopped worshiping Him as we should. Review the list of examples of sinful refuges on page 94. What are your refuges? Remember, a refuge can even be something good—but something you have given a sinful emphasis.

8. Carefully follow the steps listed in the chapter for forsaking an idol, and document your actions here. Formulate an effective plan for guarding against this idol in the future.

9. Read the following verses. Does your heart share the passion for God that these biblical writers had?

    a)   Psalm 42:1-2

    b)   Psalm 86:11-12

    c)   Psalm 119:2b

    d)   Psalm 119:10

    e)   Psalm 119:46, 69

    f)   Matthew 6:33-34

    g)   2 Corinthians 5:9

    h)   Philippians 3:10

Chapter Eight

A Husband's Responsibility
Love

Love is essential to the Christian walk. When Jesus was asked what the greatest commandment was, He said it was to love God with all our heart and to love our neighbor as ourselves (Matthew 22:37-40). But with all the misconceptions about love around, we need to define love as God does, putting off the counterfeit love of the world and putting on biblical love. The standard of Christlike love is high, but it alone is the kind of love that can make an exemplary husband.

1. Read 1 John 3:16 and 4:19. Why is it necessary to know God before you can truly love your wife (or anyone else)?

2. List the eight false conceptions about love found in the world today. Which of these worldly understandings have you found in your own life?

3. Read through the "Characteristics of Love" listed in the chapter. What are the three characteristics that are most lacking in your love for your wife? Write out a plan for biblical change (confess, repent, put off, put on) for each of these three. If necessary, enlist the help of a mature Christian brother to hold you accountable.

4. Write out a definition of love in your own words. Explain what this means specifically for your marriage relationship.

5. Prayerfully read over the put off/put on lists in the chapter. These deal with proud, arrogant, fearful, bitter, and preoccupied attitudes and actions. List all of those thoughts and behaviors of which you are guilty. List the loving replacement for each, and plan to implement them with your wife today.

Chapter Nine

A Husband's Responsibility
Leadership – Part I

Your leadership as a husband is a mandate from God, and as such is a privilege and a responsibility. Christ's way of leading is very different from worldly leadership and the fleshly leadership that comes so naturally. While poor leadership is the cause of many conflicts in marriage, good leadership can help bring peace and direction into marriage. We can learn all we need to know about how to be God's kind of leaders in the home by looking at Christ's perfect example in Scripture.

1. What is the critical difference between natural leadership and spiritual leadership? Hint: What is the focus of each type?

2. What are the three important qualifications (that is, restrictions) concerning the authority God has given you as a husband?

3. Summarize, in your own words, each of the characteristics of good shepherd-leadership. Choose one or two characteristics that are most lacking in your life and write out what you need to do to improve.

4. In your own words, explain what it means to lord your leadership over your wife. In what ways have you been guilty of doing this to your wife?

5. In what ways have you let your wife take leadership in your home? Carefully plan a discussion with your wife (based on the instructions in the chapter) to begin the process of reassuming your God-given role of leader.

Notes

Chapter Ten

A Husband's Responsibility
Leadership – Part II

The fear of decision-making seems to be one of the biggest reasons husbands are reluctant to lead. A husband may have a struggle with the fear of failure, the fear of rejection, or the fear of the unknown. For many, decision-making is a very confusing and frustrating process that they would rather just ignore. This is a topic that has been extremely muddied by man's opinion and practices. Even in the Christian community, husbands are receiving the wrong information about decision-making. This problem is caused by an overall lack of biblical thinking and discernment. Discernment is the ability or commitment to evaluate all ideas and practices by the objective truth of God (Proverbs 2:1-13; Philippians 1:9-11). Jay Adams in his book, *A Call to Discernment*, writes:

> Lack of discernment is one of the principal problems that pastors face. . . . In every area of life, members of the church are continually bombarded with ideas, beliefs, and opinions, most of which are unbiblical or at least biblically suspect. . . . Often the church itself contributes to the problem by sending conflicting and erroneous messages. Truly confusion reigns. (Jay E. Adams, *A Call to Discernment*, Eugene, OR: Harvest House, 1987, pp. 11-12)

Most of us have used various wrong methods of decision-making over the years. As a result of all the confusion, many husbands have questions that remain unanswered, such as:

1. As the leader of your family, you must know what your direction and goals are. Review the five goals listed in the chapter and apply those goals specifically to your family. Write them out and discuss them with your wife, then work toward implementing them together.

2. List the five areas which you should be overseeing in your wife's life. For each area, note at least two things you need to improve upon.

3. Think of an area in which your wife is struggling and in which you should be leading her better. Determine what you need to do for each of the following five steps detailed in the chapter so that this will be a God-honoring and spiritually profitable experience.

a) Do adequate data gathering: observe, talk to your wife, and study the Scriptures.
b) Pray for biblical wisdom.
c) Think through the proper approach: how severe should it be, remembering that it must be as gracious and gentle as possible?
d) Have the right goals: do you really want to glorify God and do your wife good?
e) Be prepared to graciously explain your reasoning and God-honoring goals if your wife continues to disagree.

4. If your wife is unsaved, answer the following questions:
   a) Are you a godly witness by example more than by words? In what ways could your wife accuse you of hypocrisy because your actions do not match your profession?

   b) Do you regularly demonstrate that your love for her places her interests above your own? In what way can you improve on preferring your wife so that your testimony of Christ will be emphasized?

   c) Are there any outstanding sin issues between you and your wife? Go to her today and acknowledge the sin, seek her forgiveness, and demonstrate to her that you are changing your ways.

Read also Study Guide Appendices 4-7 before answering the following questions.

5. What is the difference between God's decretive will and God's preceptive will? Which one are you responsible to diligently seek out and follow?

6. Consider the "Subjective Means of Making Decisions" in this chapter. Of which of these are you guilty? Give an example of when you made a decision subjectively rather than basing it on biblical principles.

7. Discuss briefly why the biblical presuppositions of decision-making are so crucial to God-honoring decisions.

8. What is the first step to biblical decision-making?

9. After data gathering, what are the three basic considerations of biblical decision-making?

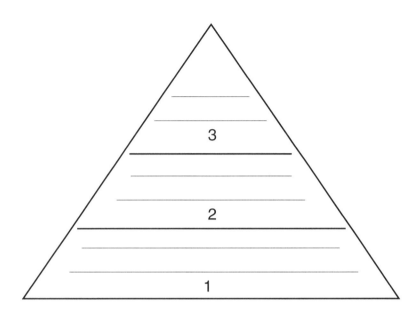

10. Using the decision-making form in Study Guide Appendix 7, work through a current decision you and/or your wife need to make.

Notes

Chapter Eleven

A Husband's Responsibility
Physical Intimacy

God created physical intimacy in marriage as a rich blessing. But the world has confused and degraded sex and made it a primary means of gratifying the lusts of the flesh. As in every area of your relationship with your wife, unselfish service in your sex life, with attention given to your wife's desires, will be a joyous, pure expression of your love. When you and your wife have the right perspective of physical intimacy, you will enjoy it to the fullest and bring glory to God.

1. Sex is not the basis for marriage, but it is still very important to the marriage relationship. What are the three reasons why sex is important? Provide a Scripture reference for each of the three.

2. Read 1 Corinthians 7:3. What principle does this verse teach for sexual intimacy in marriage?

3. Schedule a time when you and your wife can be alone. Have a talk with her to find out about her sexual desires. Discuss the following questions:
    a) How strongly does she think and feel about having sex? How often?
    b) What does she like the most? Include the time leading up to intimacy (what "gets her in the mood"), foreplay (what brings her along), and satisfaction (what brings her the most pleasure). Make a list of these things if necessary.
    c) What does she dislike? Make sure you understand her answer so you can stop doing those things.

4. Sexual intimacy is the expression of a loving relationship between a husband and wife. Review the six suggestions under principle #4 for making your relationship the basis for sexual intimacy. Which of these are in need of improvement in your marriage? Plan to implement them the next time you and your wife have sex.

Chapter Twelve

A Husband's Responsibility Stewardship

How we handle the resources God gives us says much about our maturity and character. Unless we learn to become faithful stewards, we will not be able to fulfill our responsibilities as husbands. Good stewardship is a necessary path toward usefulness to God. He has given us so much, but that only increases our obligation to look at those gifts closely and see how we can best use them to glorify Him.

1. What is stewardship? Write a definition in your own words.

2. Read Psalm 24:1; 1 Corinthians 4:7; and James 1:17. What important truth do these verses teach you concerning earthly possessions and relationships?

3. Go back over the "Hindrances to Faithful Stewardship" listed in the chapter. Which of these sins are a problem for you? What can you do today to repent and put on righteous behavior in their place?

4. Read the list of twelve convictions we must have about time. Which of these convictions need to be solidified in your life? Write them down and meditate on the Scripture provided with each one.

5. Which of the suggestions under the heading "Getting a handle on the use of your time" would be most helpful to you in seeking to be a wise steward of your time (see also Appendix 7 in *The Exemplary Husband*)? Ask someone to keep you accountable to follow these suggestions.

6. Read the list of eleven convictions we must have about money. Are there any that you have not been faithful in? Write them down and meditate on the Scripture provided with each one.

7. Which of the "Suggestions for taking control of your finances" would be most helpful to you in seeking to be a wise steward of your money (see also Appendix 8 in *The Exemplary Husband*)?

Chapter Thirteen

A Husband's Resolve
Humility and Service

Humility is central to our Christian life, and our role as husbands. We cannot come to God nor love Him supremely without it. We cannot love and serve our wives without it. Pride, humility's enemy, is the defining characteristic of those who do not know God. The natural man's bent is toward self, self-focus, self-service, self-love. Pride can easily infect our lives as Christians if we are not diligent to be rid of it. And the more we indulge pride, the more blind we become to it. To uproot our pride, we must have repentant hearts, look at ourselves through the lens of Scripture, and especially look to Christ, the greatest example of humility.

1. Review the section of this chapter on "A Definition of Pride." Why is pride such a serious sin?

2. It is easy to see the pride in one who is arrogant, but what about those who are caught up in self-pity or "low self-esteem"? How is this mindset also a proud one?

3. Carefully review the 30 examples of prideful attitudes and behaviors in this chapter. List 10 of them that apply to you. Rank them in order, beginning with the biggest pride problem. Write out and implement a plan for biblical change in these areas, beginning with the first and most severe problem.

4. Read each of the following passages and briefly explain how each one contributes to a proper view of self.

    a) Psalm 8:1-4

    b) Romans 3:10-18; John 15:5

    c) 1 Corinthians 4:7; James 1:17

    d) Ephesians 2:4-7; Romans 5:6-8

5. Read Mark 10:45; Luke 22:25-27; Philippians 2:5-11. What principle concerning humility did Jesus teach by example?

6. Review the list of 25 manifestations of humility in the chapter. Compare your "top-ten list" of proud attitudes and behaviors in your life. Which manifestations of humility will help you defeat pride in your life?

7. Study James 4:7-10. List at least seven commands in this passage which are steps to humbling yourself.

Chapter Fourteen

A Husband's Resolve
Sensitivity

It's common for men to joke about the impossibility of understanding their wives. But God commands us to understand our wives (1 Peter 3:7), which means, despite any difficulty, He has given us the means to attain it. It remains to us to work hard at achieving that goal. We must often ask ourselves (and our wives) whether we are living with them in an understanding way, and then take specific steps to grow in that understanding.

1. How does the cultural view of women in Peter's day compare with the cultural view of women today?

2. How well do you know your wife? Ask her what she thinks of your knowledge of her.

3. If you were to be tested on your knowledge of her, how would you really fare?

4. What specific ways can you grow in your knowledge of her?

5. What is your specific plan for gaining knowledge and an understanding of her?

6. In what ways do you show honor towards your wife? Ask her what would go a long way in improving in this area.

Chapter Fifteen

A Husband's Resolve
Helping His Wife Deal With Her Sin

As your wife's spiritual leader, it is your responsibility before God to help your wife deal with her sin biblically. You cannot sanctify her, but you can exhort and encourage her in her goal of Christlikeness. Unfortunately, many husbands are all too eager to harshly judge and criticize their wives when they sin. Instead we must be loving, humble, prayerful, and careful as we shepherd our wives. We must be more concerned for our own sin and motives for helping them than about what our wives do or don't do. And we must be examples to them in dealing with sin in our own lives.

1. What does it mean to make your wife a "sanctification project"? Why is this wrong, and how will you guard against this?

2. In deciding which of your wife's sins to address, you must understand what "love covers a multitude of sins" means.

    a) Explain from the chapter what it means to "cover" a sin.

    b) Given that understanding, what does the phrase "love covers a multitude of sins" mean? What does it not mean?

3. What are the three principles for dealing with sin graciously?

4. Formulate a plan that details what you will do the next time you see your wife commit a clear sin that is not a pattern for her (Example One).

5. What are the important principles to remember if your wife is unrepentant after you confront her sin?

6. Review the characteristics of "Shallow Remorse" in this chapter. Which of these are a problem for you? Begin practicing godly sorrow and repentance so that God will be glorified and your wife will be helped by your example.

7. Are there any areas of bitterness between you and your wife? Take the initiative to sit down with her and walk through this chapter's plan to remove bitterness from your marriage.

Notes

Chapter Sixteen

A Husband's Resolve
Good Communication

One of the chief complaints husbands and wives make about their spouses is that they don't communicate. A marriage is only as good as a couple's ability to send and receive the right message. But beyond its effect on the marriage, good communication is important to God. Look carefully at how you communicate, because your communication will reveal the kind of man you are. Poor, sinful communication habits must be replaced with those that please God. Unless you truly desire to honor God in this aspect of your marriage, the relationship will never be what it could be.

1. What is the key principle about our communication that is taught by Matthew 12:34?

2. What are the six prerequisites for good communication?

3. In which of these prerequisites are you the weakest? Be aware of this weakness and seek to improve as you communicate with your wife and others.

4. What are the four characteristics of good communication? Briefly define and give a Scripture reference for each.

Chapter Seventeen

A Husband's Resolve
Conflict Resolution

Differences of opinion between husband and wife are perhaps inevitable, but conflict is not. Conflict is the sinful response to differences or offenses. God hates conflict, and wants us to have no part in it. The Bible is full of commands about controlling our words and our spirit, full of warnings about strife, and full of instruction on what to do if someone is angry with us or sinning against us. Every exemplary husband can and must know how to biblically avoid and resolve conflicts with his wife.

1. One source for conflict in your marriage will be the differences between you and your wife. List at least five areas of difference between you and your wife that can cause conflict.

2. How can you deal with differences in order to avoid conflict?

3. Read James 4:1-3 again. What does James say about the cause of sinful conflict?

4. List several of the lusts in your life that cause you to engage in conflict with your wife.

5. What biblical principle is represented by these diagrams?

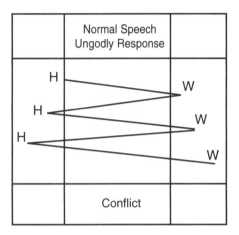
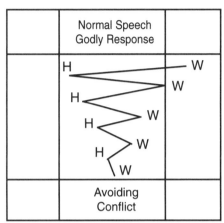

(Used by permission from Zondervan Publishers House (Grant ID:21910), out of *The Christian Counselors Manual* by Jay Adams, pg. 357-358, Grand Rapids, Michigan, 1973.)

6. Review the four sinful ways to avoid conflict. Which of these are you most often guilty of? Use the list of God-honoring ways to avoid conflict as you plan how you will deal with the next conflict that arises between you and your wife.

7. Using the chapter's guidelines for resolving a conflict biblically, write out a plan for resolving one of the conflicts you are currently having with your wife. Show the list of guidelines to your wife as well, so she will understand your approach.

Chapter Eighteen

A Husband's Regret
Anger

Anger has been redefined in our day as frustration, stressing out, blowing off steam, venting, or any number of other euphemisms. But as Christians we must understand anger for what it really is: a sin against God that Christ put on par with murder (Matthew 5:21-22). Sinful anger controls many men today and as a result marriages are severely damaged. As we strive to be exemplary husbands, we must put off sinful anger, understanding where it manifests itself in our lives, whether it is the violent and explosive or the slow-burning kind. Once that anger is put off, it must be replaced with gentleness, patience, and humility.

1. What is the difference between righteous anger and unrighteous anger?

2. In what ways do you express unrighteous anger?

3. Go back and answer the questions to the Examination section of this chapter.

4. Begin working on your desires and thoughts behind these angry displays. Write them out. Use the "Taking Thoughts Captive" worksheet in Appendix 1 of *The Exemplary Husband* to help you.

5. Begin a study of the patience and long-suffering of God. Ask your pastor where you can find helpful resource material on these topics.

6. Who else might help assist you in holding you accountable with regard to replacing your anger with gentleness? Ask them if they would do this.

Chapter Nineteen

A Husband's Regret
Anxiety and Fear

Husbands have great potential for worry because they have such great responsibility. It's easy to let the pressures of life overwhelm us and take our focus off of the Lord and His peace and become consumed with our problems. But God knows the difficulties we face and He has given us the spiritual resources to combat our anxieties and fears and trust Him. Fear does not have to control us. Instead, we are commanded by God to control our fear. Through practice of His principles you can conquer a pattern of anxiety or ungodly fears.

1. Do you understand the connection between anxiety and fear? What is it?

2. What are some facts concerning ungodly fear?

3. Go back and answer the questions on the Examination section of this chapter.

4. Write down your anxious and fearful thoughts and begin working at replacing them. Use the "Taking Thoughts Captive" worksheet in Appendix 1 of *The Exemplary Husband* to help you in this exercise.

Chapter Twenty
A Husband's Regret
Lust

Lust can and will destroy a man's life and his marriage relationship as no other sin will. With our sex-obsessed society, temptations in this area are everywhere. But while the world accepts lust as normal, we as Christian husbands cannot let this sin gain even the slightest foothold in our lives. Lustful thoughts in themselves are sins, but they won't stop in our minds. If our thoughts aren't brought under control, our internal lusts will progress to more outward sin. Search your heart carefully and be vigilant to remove any traces of impure thoughts you find there.

1. Define lust. What is the difference between a good desire and an evil one?

2. List some of the lies you might have with regard to your lusts.

3. What is the opposite of lust and why?

4. Why must your lust be nipped in the bud?

5. What provisions might you be making to feed your lusts?

6. What steps will you take to walk in the Spirit?

7. Take the time to answer the section on Examination in this chapter.

8. Write down the various lusts you have and start renewing them with God's Word. Use the "Taking Thoughts Captive" worksheet in Appendix 1 of *The Exemplary Husband* to help you.

Chapter Twenty-One

When All Is Said and Done

All that we have learned and begun to practice about being exemplary husbands depends first of all on our greatest priority—our relationship with
God. We must be worshiping, maturing Christians if we want to have any
hope of being the husbands God wants us to be. Next, we need to work
continually at loving our wives. Husbands are called to love their wives as
Christ loved the Church. It's easy to feel overwhelmed by this sobering
command. But with God's help and dedicated effort we can put on
Christlike love and become godly husbands.

1. After all the Scripture you have read and thought about as it pertains to
    your life, do you have the assurance that you are a Christian? If not, or
    if you're still struggling with it, please talk with your pastor about it.

2. Would you say you are worshiping God with your whole heart and
    mind? List a few ways that your walk with Christ has grown over
    the past several weeks.

3. Do any of the excuses listed in the chapter sound familiar to you? If so, which ones? What needs to take place to replace them?

4. What steps will you take to pass these truths on to other men (2 Timothy 2:2)?

Appendix

APPENDIX 1

Some Often Used Deceptions Within the Minds of Men
Dr. Stuart W. Scott

1. The "oops" view = no big deal. It was just a mistake.
2. The "relabeled" view = I wasn't sinfully angry, I was just stressed, or frustrated, or pressured, etc.
3. The "under the bridge" view = what's past is past. We don't need to deal with it now.
4. The various "comparison" views=
   a. Compared with my past - the way I used to be - what's the problem?
   b. Compared with others and their problems - if you think I'm bad, you should look at . . .
   c. Compared to others - they're doing it, so it must be OK for me to do.
   d. Compared with all the good I do - the good far outweighs the bad.
5. The "victim" view = someone or something caused me to sin. I couldn't help it.
6. The "no one's perfect, I'm only human" view = God expects me to act like a fallen human being.
7. The "there's too much in Scripture to obey" view = surely God doesn't really expect me to obey all that is in Scripture.
8. The "it's all taken care of" view = since God paid for all my sins, past, present, and future, I don't have any responsibility to deal with my sin.
9. The "my sin doesn't affect others" view = what's private is private, my sins don't really affect others.
10. The "oh, I may as well sin in my actions" view = since I'm battling sin in my mind and not faring very well, I may as well sin in my actions.
11. The "last time" view = I'm going to go ahead and sin this time, but this will be the last time.
12. The "why are you looking at me?" view = he or she has got the log, so why are you looking at my speck?
13. The "you'd do the same, if you were in my situation" view = I'm

unique, my situation is unique, and I just had to sin.

14. The "I confessed it, so why are there consequences?" view = my acknowledging my sin and confessing it ought to remove all consequences.

15. The "I deserve the pleasures that sin offers" view = I'm not getting what I rightfully should have, so I'll sin to get it because I deserve these pleasures.

16. The "sin is not so bad, if no one is around" view = if no one else knows or sees it, it is not that serious.

17. The "God sees my heart and the desire to please Him, so He overlooks my sin" view = when I sin, God sees the good intentions that are there from time to time. If I intend to change or want to change, it's as good as change itself.

18. The "God has changed in His view and treatment of sin" view = God has certainly changed from how He viewed sin in the O.T. and is now much softer and lenient with it for His children.

19. The "I can't obey God unless someone helps me" view = I can't do right unless or until others step in and help.

20. The "kiss and make up" view = God accepts my constant ritual of acknowledging my sin and asking for forgiveness without serious thought as to repentance going on.

21. The "if we're not talking about the sin anymore, then it's not an issue any more" view = it must no longer be an issue if we aren't discussing it. Out of conversation = out of my mind and life.

APPENDIX 2

Man is Not a Victim

Many see themselves as little more than a victim of their circumstances. The truth is, *victim* is not a biblical word. Even those who are treated ruthlessly are not referred to as *victims*. There are several aspects of the word *victim* that we need to consider when addressing this view. If a person suffers an unprovoked crime or sin at the hands of someone else, the person suffering *could be* considered a victim in the sense that he is a receiver of unwarranted treatment. Our legal system will certainly designate him the victim of a crime.

But there are wrong ideas usually associated with the word *victim*. Most often, it carries with it the idea of *complete* innocence when referring to the one who has suffered the offense. This is *rarely* the case so far as the *events* are concerned and *never* the case so far as the *heart* is concerned (Psalm 14:2-3). Let me explain by way of an example.

If you are *lawfully* stopped at a traffic light when a drunk driver rear-ends your car, you are certainly legally innocent *in the accident*. The drunk person is obviously breaking the law of God and man by driving while intoxicated and by hitting you. *If*, by the grace of God, you get out of your car and help the drunk person with pure motives until an ambulance comes to examine you both (rather than yelling at him for ruining your bumper), you can still be considered spiritually *innocent in this event*. However, if you consider yourself to be a better person than the drunk, or look down at his sin in disgust, you are sinning the sin of pride and are, therefore, no longer *innocent in the event*.

I am not saying that God does not respond compassionately when we are wronged. He does (Hebrews 4:14-6; Isaiah 63:9). And, I am not saying that God will not hold the offender fully responsible. He will (Ezekiel 18:2, 20). What I am saying is that we must remember that God sees any reactionary sin on our part during an incident as grievous as well (Romans 12:14-21).

And, we must keep an offender's sin in perspective of our own sin against a Holy God.

> **But you, why do you judge your brother? Or you again,**
> **why do you regard your brother with contempt? For we**
> **will all stand before the judgment seat of God. For it is**
> **written, "as I live, says the Lord, every knee shall bow to**
> **me and every tongue shall give praise to God." So then**
> **each one of us will give an account of himself to God.**
> **Therefore let us not judge one another anymore, but rather**
> **determine this—not to put an obstacle or a stumbling block**
> **in a brother's way.**
> **Romans 14:10-13**

Most people *do* sin in response to another person's sin and most people *do* see their own sin as less offensive than another's. When we have been wronged it can be very helpful to remember that nothing anyone has done to us is worse than our own sin against a holy God. Since any good in our lives can only be accredited to God's work in us (Jeremiah 17:9; Matthew 19:17; 1 Corinthians 4:7), and since our sin was so bad that God allowed His only Son to be killed in order to pay for our sin (2 Corinthians 5:21; 1 Corinthians 15:3), we know that we are *not* in and of ourselves any better than any one else because we sin on a regular basis.

> **But now apart from the Law the righteousness of God has**
> **been manifested, being witnessed by the Law and the**
> **Prophets, even the righteousness of God through faith in**
> **Jesus Christ** *for all those who believe; for there is no distinc-*
> *tion; for all have sinned and fall short of the glory of God.*
> **Romans 3:21-23 [emphasis mine]**

Secondly, the word *victim* can imply that a "senseless, never-should-have-happened" event has taken place. The danger here is to forget the loving sovereignty (perfect and purposeful control) of God in one's life. While some events may indeed be tragic, God knows the end from the beginning and how that event can serve to humble a person (Job 42:1-6), draw a person to Himself (John 6:44), show Himself to be a greater-than-anything God (Jeremiah 32:17; Genesis 50:20) and/or reveal Himself to the sufferer as

Refuge, Strength and Helper (Isaiah 57:15).

In short, only God has the ability to work all things together for both our good *and* His glory in a fallen world, never ignoring one to achieve the other. We must not take the view that something shouldn't have happened to us. Is God not good? Is God wrong? Is God lacking in power? Obviously none of these are true according to the Bible.

> **And we know that God causes all things to work together**
> **for good to those who love God, to those who are called**
> **according to His purpose.**
> **Romans 8:28**

Thirdly, the word *victim* often gives a person a hopeless outlook. No one who knows God is without hope, the ability to overcome and the resources to live with joy and thankfulness in spite of what has happened. This must sometimes be taken on faith until the truth and principles of God's Word can be specifically applied to one's situation and thinking (Genesis 50:20; John 20:24-29; 1 Corinthians 10:13; 1 Peter 1:6-7). Unfortunately, some individuals have been taught that they can never lead "normal" lives again. This is tragic because it utterly contradicts Scripture.

> **Grace and peace be multiplied to you in the knowledge of**
> **God and of Jesus our Lord; seeing that His divine power** *has*
> *granted to us everything pertaining to life and godliness,*
> **through the true knowledge of Him who called us by His**
> **own glory and excellence. For by these He has granted to us**
> **His precious and magnificent promises,** *so that by them you*
> *may become partakers of the divine nature,* **having escaped**
> **the corruption that is in the world by lust.**
> **2 Peter 1:2-4 [emphasis mine]**

Finally, the word *victim* usually allows a person to ignore personal responsibility. That brings us back to where we started. To be "a victim of your circumstances" is to declare yourself free from responsibility so far as thoughts, actions, usefulness and life direction are concerned. If we cannot help our responses, we conveniently cannot be held accountable for them. I have heard such statements as, "My sin is actually the result of a 'sickness' that I have because of what happened to me," "I am this way because of my parent's failures," "I turned out this way because we were poor and I was exposed to many bad influences; I didn't have a chance," or " I have a disease or chemical imbalance; that's why I had to sin."

This blame-shifting (whether subtle or not) is a grievous thing to my heart. I listen to these people as they seek to excuse themselves for their sin, knowing that at the same time they are removing all hope for themselves. Very often, people have been encouraged in these wrong beliefs by unbiblical counsel (which can even be "Christian" counsel). The truth is, we *will* be held accountable for our every thought, word, and deed.

> **So then each one of us will give an account of himself to God.**
> **Romans 14:12**

The Bible clearly teaches that we are always responsible for our *own* sin, no matter what our circumstances are—*not* for the sin of others, but for our *own* sin. We cannot say that "so and so" causes us to do what we do. Our own sinful heart simply is given *opportunity* to express itself in our difficult situations. We sin in response to these situations because sin is in us and because we choose to sin. Christians have a double responsibility because through salvation and the application of the Word of God, we don't *have* to sin.

> *For he who has died is freed from sin.* **Now if we have died with Christ, we believe that we shall also live with Him, knowing that Christ, having been raised from the dead, is never to die again; death no longer is master over Him. For the death that He died, He died to sin once for all; but the life that He lives, He lives to God. Even so consider yourselves to be** *dead to sin,* **but alive to God in Christ Jesus.**
> **Romans 6:7-11 [emphasis mine]**

Many times the word *victim* allows a person to think of himself wrongly. When a person adopts *the victim mentality*, he usually develops self-pitying, self-righteous, or hopeless attitudes. Those who *know God* and *abide* in His truth *can* lead the kind of life that God intended, even if they have been greatly wronged. They simply must learn to apply the word of God to their circumstances.

> **And God is able to make all grace abound to you, so that always having all sufficiency in everything, you may have an abundance for every good deed.**
> **2 Corinthians 9:8**

Notes

APPENDIX 3

Put Off I need to stop…	Put On I need to start…	When I need to practice…	Thoughts I need to renew…	Where Temptation Begins I need to avoid…
Action:	Action:			
Evidences:	Evidences:			
Verses:	Verses:			

Notes

APPENDIX 4

Key Definitions For Biblical Decision-Making

Before we can begin to understand how God's will and our choices fit together, we must clearly and biblically define the terms that apply to the topic of decision-making. Some of these terms may be different from what you have heard or have always thought. Some of them may not have entered your mind at all. Carefully read through these terms and the Scriptures that support them so we can begin on common ground.

God's Decretive Will is everything that God ordains (decides, plans) to happen. God's decreed will is a very detailed and predetermined plan (Psalm 119:16; Acts 2:23). This is God's secret plan for the most part. Though many people try to ascertain God's decretive will ahead of time, we can only know it for sure *after* it happens. For instance, you can know with absolute certainty that God decreed for you to marry your wife because the marriage ceremony actually took place. On occasion, God has chosen to reveal His decretive will (ahead of time) through Old Testament or early Church prophets. These instances are recorded in the Bible as *future prophecy*.

> **Remember the former things long past, for I am God and there is no other; I am God, and there is no one like Me, declaring the end from the beginning, and from ancient times things which have not been done, saying, "My purpose will be established, and I will accomplish all My good pleasure."**
> **Isaiah 46:9-10**

Sovereignty is the sum total of the attributes of God that allow Him to rule over and control all things with absolute perfection (authority, power, knowledge, wisdom, righteousness). Because God is completely sovereign, His decretive will is *always* accomplished and anything that is not within His plan *does not* happen. This means that whatever actually happens is part of His decreed will. Even sin is a part of His plan, in that He plans to allow it. We know that God is not the author of sin (James 1:3) but He perfectly and wisely chooses to *withhold His restraining influence over sinful hearts* in situations when He can use it to accomplish His good and perfect purposes. For those who love God, He is always working His best in their lives (Romans 8:28). We are still held responsible for our sinful choices, however, because they are *our own* sinful choices from *our own* sinful hearts. Knowing that all the events in our lives and all the choices we make fall under the sovereignty of God can be very reassuring as long as you trust that He is an all-wise and good God who is afflicted when we are afflicted (Isaiah 63:9) and who is willing to assist us in our trouble (Genesis 50:20; Isaiah 41:10; Isaiah 46:11; Proverbs 21:1; 20:24).

God's Preceptive Will is God's moral, lawful, and directional will that He sets forth *in the Bible* for us to follow. It is *revealed* through direct command and through precept (biblically-derived principles). We can know God's preceptive will *ahead of time* because it has already been revealed to us in the Bible. For instance, you can know that you are in the will of God when you choose a legal job over an illegal one, because God tells us in His Word to obey the governing authorities (Romans 13:1-2). The more we know God's revealed will and obey it, the more we will be within the will of God as a husband (Psalm 119:1-4).

The Providence of God is the secret and purposeful working out of God's decreed will by God, through the orchestrating of all events and people. God is so powerful and so complex that He can cause or prevent whatever His perfect plan prescribes for every person any given day, hour and minute. This means that whatever God allows in your life as a husband is for a specific purpose (Ephesians 1:11).

Mysticism is subjectivity applied to the spiritual realm. It is believing that spiritual reality and truth are verifiable by inward feelings, judgment, and experience. It is also believing that one has a special receiving line or *method of communication* coming from God even though that method is not substantiated by God's Word. For example, a person who believes that God wants him to join a particular church because he felt warm and tingly inside when he thought of it is an example of a mystical person. This person believes that God is communicating with him in a "special" way.

> The Christian should reject mystical experiences, because God
> has chosen to relate to man by means of man's mind, not
> through his emotions. The Word, which must be understood,
> is the ultimate [test] of truth. Subjective experience is not an
> adequate basis by which to judge the truth of anything.
> When the mystical experience is said to be a revelation from
> God, this must also be rejected. (Arthur L. Johnson, *Faith
> Misguided, Exposing the Dangers of Mysticism*. Chicago, IL:
> Moody Press, 1988, p. 41)

Husband, guard against the temptation to devise a mystical means of
communication with God (Colossians 2:8-9).

Wisdom is biblical knowledge practically applied to a holy end. Wisdom
usually concerns a collection of truths, rather than a single fact. It helps us
to discern God's perspective of all ideas, decisions and practices. God
promises to give us the wisdom we need to *understand and apply His truth* to
our decisions, but we must earnestly pray in faith and we must search His
Word. This is how we know what to do. You should not ask God to mystically reveal to you what he wants you to do (Psalm 19:7; James 1:5; 3:13-18).

Notes

APPENDIX 5

Biblical Decision-Making Presuppositions

You must begin the biblical decision-making process with some crucial presuppositions. A presupposition is what you assume to be true and therefore act upon. The following are biblical truths that you must be convinced of before you will make decisions biblically. Carefully consider these presuppositions and think about your own assumptions about decision-making before you use the following.

1. *We do not need to know God's decreed will and how He is providentially bringing it about before we make a decision.* **We are *never* told to *search for* or to *try and ascertain* God's decreed (circumstantial) will or to *interpret* God's providence for decision-making**. These are secret things, belonging only to God. Instead, we must trust that He is in control and that He is good. God wants you to determine His will in *another* way. There is only one way for us to know the mind of God— by what He has revealed in His Word. This truth means that you do not have to figure out whether or not God has decreed for you to move before you can make the right decision about moving (Isaiah 55:8-9).

   The secret things belong to the Lord our God, but the things revealed belong to us and to our sons forever, that we may observe all the words of this law.
   Deuteronomy 29:29

2. *The Holy Spirit's role is to convict, teach and conform us—all through the vehicle of the Word of God.* **We are *never* given any promise or instruction that He will *subjectively reveal* to us God's decreed (circumstantial) will**. This truth means that you should not expect some mystical direction from God to determine whether or not you should talk to your wife about an issue.

But the Helper, the Holy Spirit, whom the Father will send in My name, He will teach you all things, and bring to your remembrance all that I said to you. . . . And He, when He comes, will convict the world concerning sin and righteousness and judgment.
John 14:26; 16:8

3. *God only guides or leads his people today: (1) by providence (we know it after the fact) and (2) by Scripture (we can know it before we act).* This truth means that you can stop trying to decipher signs and feelings.

   With Your counsel You will guide me, and afterward receive me to glory.
   Psalm 73:24

   Many plans are in a man's heart, but the counsel of the Lord will stand.
   Proverbs 19:21

4. *God is a gracious God who has provided everything we need to do what He wants us to do.* The Bible is sufficient to guide us in all matters of eternal life and godliness (sanctification) including decision-making. Therefore, **it offers enough insight for us to make *every* decision a God-honoring one**. This truth means that God is not hiding His will from you and that you *can* know it.

   Your word is a lamp to my feet and a light to my path.
   Psalm 119:105

   Seeing that his divine power has granted to us everything pertaining to life and godliness, through the true knowledge of Him who called us by His own glory and excellence.
   2 Peter 1:3

5. *God holds us fully responsible to search out and follow His preceptive will (God's written Word) in all of life.* This truth means that **we as husbands will be held responsible for making all our decisions by weighing the objective (factual, outside ourselves) Word of God**.

> This book of the law shall not depart from your mouth, but
> you shall meditate on it day and night, so that you may be
> careful to do according to all that is written in it; for then
> you will make your way prosperous, and then you will have
> success.
>
> Joshua 1:8

6. *If we make a decision based on biblical commands and principles alone we can
   fully trust that **we are pleasing God** in our decision and fully trust that He
   will providentially (by circumstances out of our control) **change** our choice if it
   is not within His decreed will.* This truth means that you don't have to
   second-guess yourself anymore.

   > I have chosen the faithful way; I have placed Your ordi-
   > nances before me.
   >
   > Psalm 119:30

   > The mind of man plans his way, but the Lord directs his
   > steps.
   >
   > Proverbs 16:9

7. *To **rightly interpret** and apply the Word of God we must use a prayerful,
   literal, historical, contextual, and grammatical method of studying it.* This
   truth means that if your Bible has been on the shelf, it's time to dust it
   off! If you read your Bible, but you don't really study it and meditate
   on it, it's time to get busy! Two helpful books on how to study the Bible
   are: *How to Interpret the Bible,* by Richard Mayhue (Christian Focus
   Publications) and *How to Get the Most From Your Bible*, by John F.
   MacArthur (Word Publications).

   > Be diligent to present yourself approved to God as a work-
   > man who does not need to be ashamed, accurately handling
   > the word of truth.
   >
   > 2 Timothy 2:15

   > But know this first of all, that no prophecy of Scripture is a
   > matter of one's own interpretation.
   >
   > 2 Peter 1:20

8. *No one is ever outside of God's decreed plan.* **We cannot miss the decreed will of God** because God is sovereign. This truth means that you can stop regretting that you didn't choose the other job once you have confessed any *wrong* way you may have decided. All is not lost.

APPENDIX 6

Subjectivity and Decision-Making

Some Christians make poor decisions because they do not understand that God no longer communicates His will outside the pages of Scripture. They read the Old Testament and assume that God guides the average believer today in much the same way that He guided His people before His written Word was in existence. Some people also believe that God will individually speak to them because He spoke individually to His special prophets and Apostles. From the New Testament, however, we understand that God communicated to these individuals in special ways, *in order* to provide us with the all-sufficient and eternal Word of God (2 Peter 1:21, 1 Thessalonians 2:13). Once the Word of God was complete there was no more need for such individual communication. In fact, once the Apostles were verified as the final authentic spokesmen for God, all individual communications from God ceased (2 Peter 2:19; Hebrews 1:1-2). Read what the Westminster Confession of Faith states:

> The whole counsel of God concerning all things necessary for his own glory, man's salvation, faith *and life*, is either expressly set down in Scripture, or by good and necessary consequences may be deduced from Scripture: unto which nothing at any time is to be added, whether by new revelations of the Spirit, or traditions of men. (Emphasis mine, *The Westminster Standards, Confession of Faith*, Ch. I, VI; Philadelphia, Penn., The Great Commission Publications, 1989)

Just because God no longer communicates with us *individually*, however, does not mean that He does not communicate to us *personally* today. His written Word to us is very *personal communication* (John 16:13-15). The Holy Spirit's job is to make it even more *personal* (1 Corinthians 2:12-13). Some will strongly argue that God has individually spoken to them in one way or another, but there is no way for them to verify or trust the source of their experience, not even for themselves. Only God knows the true source of whatever they believe they have received. Just because they are *fully convinced* does not mean that they see things as they really are. Many deluded individuals have heard voices or become fully convinced of things that are clearly not true. We must measure our experiences by the objective word of God and not vice versa (e.g., Deuteronomy 13:1-4). J. I. Packer once wrote, "Wrong ideas about God's guidance lead to wrong conclusions about the right thing to do" (J. I. Packer, *Hot Tub Religion*, Wheaton, IL; Tyndale House Publishers, 1987, p. 109).

Some people make decisions subjectively because this is the norm for our society. Many people are feelings oriented. Most even use the term "feel" in place of "believe" or "think" (e.g., "How do you 'feel' about...?"). One of the reasons our society has become subjective is because it has an aversion to absolutes. For a person who does not want to recognize the Bible as the authoritative Word of God, any way of making decisions would be a better one than making decisions based on the Bible. Also, man's flesh has a natural bent towards doing things the easy way. Certainly it is easier to live life by feelings and/or signs, rather than by the hard work of engaging the mind in study. Naturally, the undisciplined and lazy person will not want to give the time or mental effort it takes to make a biblical decision. God's way of doing things is rarely the easy way, but His way always results in the greatest reward (Galatians 6:9).

Making decisions by subjective means will usually result in disappointment or even disaster. We must be sure that our way of deciding what to do is not based on former ways that God used to deal with His people (Hebrews 1:1-2), on our imaginations (Ezekiel 13:2-3, 7), on something that *seems* miraculous (Deuteronomy 13:1-4), or on our own selfish desires (Proverbs 14:12; 18:1-2).

> **"Son of man, prophesy against the prophets of Israel who prophesy, and say to those who prophesy from their own inspiration, 'Listen to the word of the Lord!' Thus says the Lord God, 'Woe to the foolish prophets who are following their own spirit and have seen nothing. . . . Did you not see a false vision, and speak a lying divination when you said, "The Lord declares," but it is not I who have spoken?'"**
> **Ezekiel 13:2-3, 7**

Subjective means of making decisions:

1. Misusing the Bible: This method involves trying to obtain biblical direction by the *open-the-Bible-and-point* method or by looking for a message from God in your daily Bible reading that will mystically tell you what He wants you to do. Both of these methods take God's Word out of its context. Instead we need to study God's Word rightly to understand the *one thing* that He meant and apply that truth to our lives. Hopefully this is not the way you decided to marry your spouse.

2. Personal advice: This is using what others think for direction when it is not founded upon biblical principles but rather on opinion and experience alone. Advice from those who are godly enough to tell you what God does and doesn't say about the matter can be very valuable, however. Either way, never use personal advice *alone* to make your decisions. A man might find himself changing jobs or churches every few months by always being swayed by others' opinion and experience (Psalm 1:1-2; Proverbs 14:12; 25:19; Isaiah 55:8-9).

3. Circumstances/results: This is assuming that you can understand what God wants you to do by reading or interpreting certain circumstances or results. Many grave mistakes have been made based on what the circumstances "seemed to say." There was once a man who experienced great confusion from reading the circumstances in order to determine if he should become a missionary. At one point the circumstances began to say, "You've made a mistake." He was turned down by three mission boards. He was even more confused when the people he was finally able to minister to never responded to his missionary efforts. The Bible teaches us that sometimes God's path is not easy. Also God often sent prophets to people that did not listen. There is no way to be certain what circumstances or results mean (Numbers 20:8-12; Joshua 9; Proverbs 13:16).

4. Setting up conditions: This is imposing a condition on God for direction. If the condition comes true then one considers that God has communicated His answer. This mystical means of decision-making is similar to reading circumstances, only with a presumptuous (assuming on or testing God) twist. For lack of trust in God's faithfulness to do what

He said He would do, Gideon of the Bible did this very thing by laying out a wool fleece for God to give him a sign on (Judges 6:36-40). Because God was merciful to Gideon at a time when His written Word was not complete, this does not mean that we can assume that it is okay to put God to the test. A husband who uses this method might tell God, "If You want me to go back to school, have someone call me in the next hour and tell me it is a good idea." He might even use spiritual lingo like, "Lord, I'm going to trust you for..." (Matthew 4:5; Psalm 19:13).

5. <u>Opened and closed doors:</u> This is using opportunities or the loss of an opportunity as a message from God about what you should do. In the Bible, opened and closed doors are *never* used in this way. In fact, Paul did not take one door that was opened to him even though it was acceptable (not sinful) to the Lord (2 Corinthians 2:12-13). It is usually spoken of in Scripture concerning an opportunity to share the gospel, *after* the fact—*not* as a means of determining God's direction. Assuming that an opened door is the direction of God can cause a husband to make very bad decisions and even neglect his family (Acts 14:27; 1 Corinthians 16:9).

6. <u>Ideas, inner feelings, desires and impressions:</u> This is interpreting something from *within* as the "voice" of God. Contrary to popular opinion, just because an idea, feeling, desire, etc. seems "good," this does not mean it is of God. Any one of these things from within could be from self or the Evil One. Garry Friesen writes in his book, *Decision Making and the Will of God:*

> For impressions could be produced by any number of sources: God, Satan, an angel, a demon, human emotions (such as fear or ecstasy), hormonal imbalance, insomnia, medication, or an upset stomach. ... Impressions are real; believers experience them. But impressions are *not authoritative.* (Emphasis Friesen's, Multnomah Press, Portland Oregon, 1980, pp. 130-131)

Some people believe that if they love the Lord and strongly desire something that seems good, that desire is from God. A verse that is often taken out of context is Psalm 37:4:

Delight yourself in the Lord; and He will give you the desires of your heart.

A person cannot assume that just because they love God, *every* desire they have is from Him. What this verse *does* mean is the more you delight in God, the more you will desire the right kinds of things. Feelings can be attributed to our thinking, our physical condition or our spiritual state, but not as a message from God.

Interpreting inner "signs" as God's direction could lead a husband to commit sin. A husband might even divorce his wife without biblical grounds because "God communicated that it was okay" (2 Samuel 7:1-7; Matthew 16:4; 16:21-23).

7. <u>An audible voice:</u> This is hearing a voice that is not coming from a person who is speaking to you and believing it to be the audible voice of God. *This is very dangerous.* If you are hearing voices, it is either *satanic* in origin (only possible for unbelievers) or a *personal delusion* stemming from sleep loss, a mind that knows no bounds or from living in gross sin. Even if what you "hear" seems good and right you must not assume that it is from God or that it should be acted upon. We know that God does not intend to add *anything* to His Word (Hebrews 1:1-2; 2 Peter 1:17-21).

8. <u>Misusing prayer:</u> This is believing that you can receive some sort of message from God through prayer. This is nothing more than putting stock in ideas/inner feelings/desires/ impressions that you receive while you are praying. The purpose of prayer is *not* to **receive** anything (but strength) from God but to **give** confessions, praises, thanksgiving, and petitions, to **align** our thinking with God's thinking, and to **express** our dependence and trust. Husbands, we must be sure that we are not looking for a sign or a feeling from God when we pray. When Jesus taught the disciples to pray he gave a model prayer which did not include receiving any messages from God (Luke 11:2-4). (For verses showing the fallacy of interpreting ideas, inner feelings, or desires as direction from God, see #6.)

9. <u>Inner peace:</u> This is interpreting a sense of peace or an unrest in your

soul as direction from God. This is also a feeling. We are commanded to be at peace with God (salvation). We are also commanded to be at peace in our mind (free from anxiety). We are even commanded to be at peace with one another (as much as depends on us). If we are truly not at peace, we are in sin. If someone is using the phrase "I don't have peace about it" to mean they have a gut feeling that they shouldn't do something or to mean that God is letting them know that they shouldn't do something—this is subjective and totally unreliable. If they mean, "I feel troubled about making that choice because I am thinking about certain things that concern me" or "because I don't have enough information to make a wise (or holy) decision," this is a matter of wisdom and discernment which involves factual data, God's wisdom, and the thinking process—*not just feelings*. It would be better to say, "I can't be sure that this is a wise (or holy) decision yet." This is exactly the case with Paul in 2 Corinthians 2:13. He had no "rest for his spirit" because he did not *think* it was wise to go to Troas without Titus. Paul was not saying that his unrest was a message from God. Nine times out of ten a person is "not at peace" about a decision because of something they are thinking, and they mistakenly attribute their feelings to a mystical message from God. If their feeling is not from their thinking, it could be from any number of physical or personal reasons (desires). Whether or not a person has inner peace is never used for decision-making in the Bible. When you are uneasy about a decision, determine what you are thinking about the facts that are involved or your own desires. Husband, sometimes what you feel worst about is the most right thing to do (Romans 5:1; 12:18; Philippians 4:6-9; Colossians 3:14-15).

There are varying views about the definitions, presuppositions, and methods we have discussed. Many people are not sure what they believe, which causes them to move in and out of different views. God has given us a far better way to make decisions than by these subjective means. Before a person will turn to the biblical way of making decisions, they must see the fallacy of these subjective decision-making methods. They must not trust their own judgment.

> **There is a way which seems right to a man, but its end is the way of death.**
> **Proverbs 16:25**

Every exemplary husband must acknowledge that Scripture does not support these subjective means of determining God's will. In his book, *Reckless Faith*, John MacArthur writes:

[Very] ... significant ... is the fact the *Scripture never commands us to tune into any inner voice*. We are commanded to study and meditate on Scripture (Joshua 1:8; Psalm 1:1-2). We're instructed to cultivate wisdom and discernment (Proverbs 4:5-8). We're told to walk wisely and make the most of our time (Ephesians 5:15-16). We're ordered to be obedient to God's commands (Deuteronomy 28:1-2; John 15:14). But we are never encouraged to listen for inner promptings. (Emphasis MacArthur's, p. 192, Crossway Books, Wheaton, Ill., 1994)

Notes

APPENDIX 7

Biblical Decision-Making

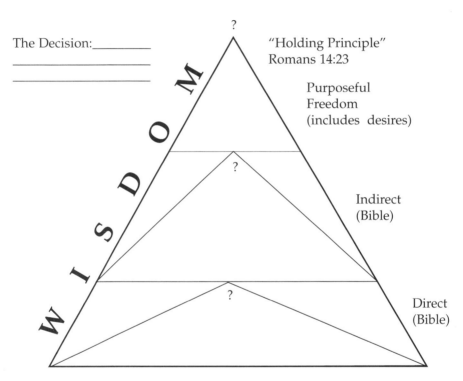

The Decision:_____
_____
_____

? "Holding Principle"
Romans 14:23

Purposeful
Freedom
(includes desires)

Indirect
(Bible)

Direct
(Bible)

WISDOM

Attitude: Prayerfully humbly, to please Christ

Any Factual Data
(Proverbs 18:13):_____
_____
_____
_____
_____

Appendix 8

Discovering Problem Patterns

Name _____

Date _____

Directions: For one week carefully list *all* events, situations or activities (good or bad) that resulted in _____.
Circle those that occur three or more times.

	Sunday	Monday	Tuesday	Wednesday	Thursday	Friday	Saturday
Morning							
Afternoon							
Evening							

(Used by permission from Zondervan Publishing House (Grant ID:), out of *The Christian Counselor's Manual* by Jay Adams pg. 280, Grand Rapids, Michigan, 1973.)